THE
DUPLICATIVE
SPONSORING SYSTEM

TO ALL NETWORK MARKETERS:

MORE PROSPECTS!
MORE MONEY!
MORE EXCITEMENT!

NQOBILE TSHUMA

Order this book online at www.trafford.com
or email orders@trafford.com

Most Trafford titles are also available at major online book retailers.

Printed in the United States of America.

ISBN: 978-1-4669-9591-8 (sc)
ISBN: 978-1-4669-9590-1 (e)

Trafford rev. 05/22/2013

www.trafford.com

North America & international
toll-free: 1 888 232 4444 (USA & Canada)
phone: 250 383 6864 ♦ fax: 812 355 4082

TABLE OF CONTENTS

INTRODUCTION

Hello and Congratulations to you for having made such a wise decision to get hold of a simple but powerful system that will mentor you on how to attract an endless number of new distributors and customers to you.

Millions of people worldwide are fast realizing that job security is a big dilema; consequently, they need to make money NOW! Even those people who are gainfully employed are more than ever, discovering that their income can hardly last them two weeks after pay day, hence they need to start a home based business. I can safely say, ONLY, the people who are going to reap benefits from this huge migration are those who have acquired the finest skills of attracting prospects to themselves. Precisely, that's what the DUPLICATIVE SPONSORING SYSTEM is all about.

This book has been written in a language so simply such that the net work marketing amatures can understand its concepts and easily apply it in their own business irregardless of the company they belong to. In fact, I strongly believe that, if you religiously follow the attraction secrets taught in this manifesto you will achieve life changing results beyond your wildest dreams. Have you ever imagined the excietment one can experience in having over 20 prospects calling you everyday and sponsoring say 10-30 new distributors per month in your primary opportunity, it sounds crazy isn`t it?—its very possible.

I have done everything it takes an average net worker to succeed:

I have attended several hotel meetings. I have maintained a contact list of over 100 names in my business diary.

I have organized business parties with my team.

I used to distribute thousands of flyers at all corners in town hoping to receive a call from a potential prospect, only to get disappointed! Then I would ask my up line why I'm I failing to sponsor new reps when I'm hard working like this. The usually response I got was:

You MUST talk to MORE people and NEVER give up!

I guarantee you that, you have grabbed this book at the correct time and more so consuming the right information that will change your life forever, as long you will follow step by step the advice given in this book. You shall be taught how to build your confidence and leadership skills through the use of the internet. This strategy will naturally compel your prospects to pre-sell themselves to you, because they see you as a valuable asset to their success.

I personal created the duplicative sponsoring system, to suit even the newbies to get off to a quick start and immediately start generating more leads, more cash as they plug into my proven system.

ENJOY YOUR READING FOR THE NEXT THREE HOURS OR SO!

CHAPTER ONE

FACTS ABOUT ATTRACTION PHILOSOPHY

Attraction system is as old as human kind. It has been there since ancient times, even during the primitive stone age there was some kind of attraction philosophy. For example, people would always love to associate with people who were physical strong for the sake of getting some form of protection from enemies. Wealth man would naturally marry many women.

During mordern times people of high credibility ranking (e.g. State Presidents, Celebrities etc) whatever they say in public is often quoted by many and it becomes an issue of public consumption. If high profile people like celebrities visit Central business district (CBD) the whole town is likely to come to a stand still as people will be rushing(attracted)to have a glance of the VIP in question.

Are these people different from us?

Do they possess a supernatural power than us?

Or should we say, they have an inherent ability to draw crowds to themselves?

NONE OF THE ABOVE.

The only attribute popular figures have is that, they are perceived as having high personal value, they can subconsciously or consciously impact to others(ie followers). Once One has something valuable to offer to the associates or society, you suddenly become an outstanding figure worth to be followed(LEADER) because people strongly feel that they can benefit from what you offer.

It is also natural that people NEED things they don't have.

So leaders are a special cut of people who are seen as being able to help others get what they don't have. Consequently, this factor alone make people gather around a leader because he or she is perceived as a *solution provider*. Hence, the reason to closely associate with him or her(attraction).

The mere fact that people have unwavering *trust* in their leader as a solution maker, it therefore follows that they are likely to buy or fall for anything that a leader puts on the table. At this juncture, we then say, one of the qualities of a leader is to have a RECOMMENDATION POWER.

If you find yourself struggling to sponsor new reps, it shows that your prospects hardly perecive you as a leader because leaders naturally attract people to themselves effortlessly. For instance, take a look at successful (top leaders) in your net work marketing company, many people (perhaps including yourself)would always wish they were signed by such people when they were initial joining the company, because people believe that by associating with top leaders can make them have a share of their power and success.

In any net work marketing company, people preach about the same:

(1) Product
(2) Marketing or compensation plan.

Surprisingly, they perform differently. The difference lies in the *distributor* and his marketing skills and how he is perceived by his audience (prospects).

This tells us that people don't join your company or your business opportunity, they join <u>YOU.</u> Then work on your personal image so that you look attractive to your prospects. The duplicative sponsoring course will teach you about how to look " better than your best" in the eyes of your prospects, using the internet(technology) as a platform.

Let's do a rewind and closely examine some of the qualities of a Leader visa-vie the net work marketing industry:

* Leaders are people who are led by their vision and dreams.
* A Leader strive for the betterment of his followers, and also radiate positive energy to the group they lead.
* When things go wrong in the team a leader accepts responsibility but when things go right he praises the team or people he leads.
* Leaders are ever learning and enhancing their knowledge, because once you stop reading you stop leading!
* They believe in the saying:

If you want to <u>fail</u> in life try to please everyone. So leaders do not care about criticism, they may easily say NO(when necessary) to someone's request without seeking that person's approval.

*   Leaders are fair and firm and they can do what the majority is not willing to do.
*   They love themselves and dress presentable.
*   They treat themselves with integrity.
*   Leaders are good listeners.
*   They humbly consult people who are more knowledgeable than them.

So let it be your habit to buy every book, cd and dvds relevant to net work marketing as this increases your personal value to others, making you attractive to your prospects.

CHAPTER TWO

GUESS WHO IS RESPONSIBLE FOR YOUR SUCCESS?

Many People in our industry think failure occurs mainly because of the poor company products or because of the ineffective marketing plan(compensation plan) or perhaps, because of bad lucky. The usually reaction is to join another company which seems to be better than the previous one. Some people change MLM Companies as if they are changing T Shirts only to realise that the situation still remains the same and get frustrated and eventually quit the business.

I personal tried over five companies in the ten years of my net work marketing adventure. suprisingly, I was meeting the same challenges in all companies, ranging from prospect's last minute cancellation of appointments to

"your products are too expensive"

and many common silly excuses

The bottom line is that YOUR BUSINESS HAS NOTHING TO DO WITH YOUR COMPANY! Your success in the business is "squarely" dependent on you the distributor, not the usually crap that

"my company is better than yours"

Our main job as reps is Marketing. He who markets best get the fattest pay cheque.

My attraction system is based on the TWO fundamental facts about human beings:

(1) people do not like to be sold anything but like to buy anything.
(2) The more valuable you are to others the more they need you.

PEOPLE DO NOT LIKE TO BE SOLD ANYTHING(products) BUT LIKE TO BUY ANYTHING (products)

when you read this statement it may sound to be contradicting itself, but lets clear the dust by having a look at a practical scenario below:

Imagine a vendor knocking on your door every day in the morning selling hand bags. At first you might welcome him but later you feel bored and perhaps start to ignore him when he knocks at your door again. Sometimes you may end up inserting a board on your door:

NO VENDORS ARE ALLOWED INTO THIS BUILDING.

Selling items to people natural pisses them off, but people would always want to buy things as long it has been their idea to do so.

Most distributors are still using the traditional approach of selling products, which include blurting out how good their company products are, as loud as they can, to whoever shall listen. What they forget is that, there are so many companies out there, making the same noise, selling simillar, QUALITY products, competing for the same market space. Moreover, people are saturated on a daily basis with sales messages from televisions, radios, cell phones etc.

So the only solution is to to create an effective marketing system that will make people think of buying products or business opportunity from you as if it is their idea to do so.

DON'T pitch your products or opportunity at first counter with your customers or prospects because they will always think you are just like an other salesman aiming at getting your hand into their pockets. So the best way to win the confidence of your customers or prospects is to build a strong relationship with them first before pitching your products or opportunity.

This does not mean you do not have to show people your products or opportunity but it means you have to earn the right to "sell" them, by first building a relationship.

If you want to sell drilling machines don't talk about drilling machines at first counter with your customers but rather advertise information about an ideal home with nice picture frames hanging on the wall so that your customer think of how can he drill the holes for hanging the picture frames. He will obviously think that they must be a device NEEDED to make holes for the picture frames. At that point, suggest that a drilling machine can be an ideal solution to his problem and you can source the device. It will appear as if it was the customer's idea to buy a drilling machine and your role was just a solution provider—just a supplier of the device.

When you position yourself as a solution provider not a sales man, you will be invited by your customers and prospects into their world as a GUEST whose sole purpose is to honestly help them not to "snatch" some money from their pockets like sales man. As a highly esteemed guest you suddenly have power and authority, so what ever you recommend to your prospects is likely to be accepted whole heartedly.

Remember:

THE FASTEST WAY OF GETTING RICH IS TO SOLVE OTHER PEOPLE'S PROBLEMS.

That's the reason why I don't initial expose my MLM opportunity to my potential prospects because its like selling them another problem, as there is possibility that, the same prospects I'm directly pitching my business opportunity to, could be involved in another MLM company and, perhaps, struggling.

THE MORE VALUABLE YOU ARE TO OTHERS THE MORE THEY NEED YOU

PLEASE note that you are NOT marketing company products or opportunity but you are marketing expertise and solutions to other people's problems(other network marketers).

The teaching or coaching aspect, proves beyond doubt, that you genuinely have the best interest of your prospects at heart, unlike others who are just trying to get their money.

Even if you honestly taught your prospect the useful information about how they can solve their problems without buying anything from you, the chances are high that, they may end up asking you questions like

"by the way sir/madam, which company do you belong to and what products do you sell?"

In this case prospects would have sold themselves to you and ready to happily give you their money.

At times they may invite you to show them your business opportunity. That way they have invited you into their world and you go there as an honourable guest not like an un invited "pest" as what normal happens when you pitch your business opportunity at the forefront to your prospects.

That's the reason why I personal teach, coach or mentor other net work markers, of which I call this process educational marketing and by so doing I have become the hunted instead of being hunter of the prospects, because they regard me as their a true valuable resource.

Let me close this chapter by a quotation from Mike Dillard, he said

"AMATEURS SELL PRODUCTS AND PUSH THEM UPON PEOPLE. PROFESSIONALS MARKET SOLUTIONS AND EXPERTISE, WHICH ATTRACT PEOPLE TOWARDS THEM"

CHAPTER THREE

CONTENT IS KING

Kindly do yourself a favor by reciting the little poem below.

People don't watch television for ads but for content.
People don't buy magazines for ads but for articles(content)
People don't buy news papers for ads but for content.
CONTENT IS KING! CONTENT IS KING!

Our primary job as distributors or reps is to _produce_ and _distribute_ educative information to our prospects. Period. End of story.

"Why, Mr. Tshuma?"

"Because people are attracted to value (content) not sales pitches."

*People watch television for content then ads are strategically placed on TV when all eyes are "glued" to the screen for the sake of content, but end up viewing ads as well.

So when you conduct your business through sales pitches (talking products & business opportunity first) without firstly educating your audience(prospects) about something that add <u>VALUE</u> to their business lives, it's like a TV station that runs adverts 24/7.

Honestly speaking, who will watch such a TV station?

The only way you can make it in this industry is to become a leader through educating others on how to run their MLM business efficiently, instead of pitching a business opportunity up front. The "coaching of others" sets you head and shoulder above any other network marketer and position you as a highly esteemed expert, thereby, attracting many prospects to you.

"Why should I prospect people already in network marketing through educating them first?"

The reply is simple:

(1) Net work marketers have a burning desire for success.
(2) MLM professionals are more than willing to buy any educational message as long as it will help them build their businesses.
(3) It is a natural disposition that people are always thirsty for leadership, so net work marketers are not an exception, they need a person like you to lead and direct them on how best they can run their businesses.

So by "teaching" them first before recruiting, you earn their trust and loyality and consequently, they can buy ANYTHING from you. It's good as selling your products to people who are ready buyers.

Precisely, I sell my company products and the business opportunity to:

* people who have decided to buy from me.
* people who decided to "sell" themselves to me.

It means the duplicative sponsoring system ensures that, I completely avoid the pain of being REJECTED by the prospects.

This is exactly the _opposite_ of what happens when one is using the traditional approach to net work marketing.

The usually "thing" is to do cold calling, inviting every body you meet in town(including relatives& friends who don't take you serious) to a weekly opportunity meeting and buying opportunity leads—the list goes on.

This approach is not all that effective because you invite EVERYBODY which may include people who are "allergic" to net work marketing and will never ever join this type of a business.

It's like playing a trial and error game, where your success is dependent on chances.

The reason why MLM professionals invite every Jack and Jick into the weekly opportunity meetings, it's because they are taught half truths that you have to prospect anyone you meet because

"everyone is your prospect"

Or "all people need your MLM opportunity, it's just that they are not yet exposed to it"

It's not true that everyone is your prospect because:

(1) Some people love their jobs such that nothing can move them out of their employment.
(2) Some people would rather be skinned alive instead of engaging in something that involves taking a risk.

(3) Some people have no desire to be entrepreneurs at all and are content working at Shell garage.

The list goes on.

Some net work marketers assume that it is their duty to change people's negative mindset about MLM opportunity. So they think that they have to persistently preach about their company opportunity to everyone until prospects change their mindset and join the business. This is the biggest mistake that most MLM proffessionals are making.

I would like to make it very clear that your duty as a net work marketer is to SHOW(not to convince people) people the opportunity and those people will then use the MLM opportunity to change themselves.

NO ONE CAN CHANGE ANYONE!

The biggest challenge facing the net work marketers is how to get the right message to the right people, who will willingly accept the MLM opportunity instead of wasting their precious time trying to recruit everybody.

The secret lies in positioning yourself as an expert whose role is to honestly educate other net work marketers on content that will help them do their business better. YOUR MOTTO SHOULD BE:

Teach them now! Earn their trust!Recruit them later!

Your prospects and your customers must BOND to you and not to your opportunity or products. So building a relationship with your target market (other net work marketers) through giving them useful information on how to work from home, does not only poses you as a trust worthy expert but it means your customers/prospects will be very loyal to you such that even if your company closes for what ever reason, you won't become a "destitute" because you can easily redirect them to a new venture.

Instead of selling products and business opportunity like other net work marketers, I sell a marketing system to other net work marketers which will in turn sell my company products and my business opportunity 24/7.

The duplicative sponsoring system I will unveil to you ensures that:

*   I generate an endless number of quality leads 24/7.
*   My prospect call me instead of me calling them.
*   People pay me for prospecting them.
*   I make serious cash from people who have decided not to join my primary opportunity.
*   People who plug into the same system can start making money as quickly as possible. The fact that new reps make immediate cash after joining the business, help to reduce the number of new distributors who quit within the first three months of joining the business.
*   The same people who have decided _NOT_ to join my opportunity are converted by my marketing system into free agents who advertise my business to other opportunity seekers(other net work markerters) _FREE OF CHARGE_. It sounds crazy man!
*   I do business presentations to thousands if not millions of people every day. It doesn't matter whether I'm dead asleep or enjoying my self in a swimming pool, I do product demos 24/7, seven days a week. How many people are you able to see per day?
*   I do business mainly by communiting from the comfort of my bedroom to my computer room.

REMEMBER:

Most people who succeed in MLM industry are those who are able to pass the company information to as many people as possible, in the shortest possible time!

So, the use of the internet is the only solution to this puzzle.

Your question could be:

How can I achieve all this, Mr Tshuma?

The answer is:

YES you can, if you simply position your self on the internet, as a leader and mentor of other net work marketers and willing to help them with the vital information on how best they can build their home based businesses.

"How. Mr Tshuma"?

"please, explain further, sir"

"No . . . wait, wait, you shall learn about it in the following chapters, as for now, just cool down"

*Who can confidently say, that working very hard is the only way of getting rich?

The truth is: working _SMART_ is the surest way of getting rich. Infact, wealthy people are the laziest people in the world, that's why the rich guys are ever devising means of working smart, but getting multiple results. Honestly, if working harder was the only way of achieving our dreams, it means people working in the construction industry could be driving potche cars, but the opposite is true.

Personal, I believe in 80% working smart and 20% working hard, perhaps, that's the reason why I sometimes do One on One business presentations to a hot prospect within my reach, but I do not entirely relay on that method.

Thats why a certain friend of mine who is a serious advocate of attraction marketing, advising MLM Professionals to opt for internet net work marketing than the traditional approach, said:

IF YOU DON'T CURRENTLY HAVE THIS KIND OF LEVERAGE IN YOUR BUSINESS . . .

INSTEAD OF TRADING HOURS FOR DOLLARS, YOU'RE TRADING HOURS FOR PROSPECTS!

The same sentiments were echored by an American billionnare Bill Gates, he said:

IF YOUR BUSINESS IS NOT ON THE INTERNET, THEN YOUR BUSINESS WILL BE OUT OF BUSINESS.

Bill Gates, Founder of Microsoft Ware.

Interesting topics that you may educate other net work marketers on, may include the following:

*   Tips on how to attract an endless number of quality leads and customers to you; without making a single call.
*   How to generate serious cash from people who have decided NOT to join your company.
*   The importance of time management to an MLM professional.
*   The top 7 mistakes that can cost you thousands.
*   Product closing skills.
*   5 "hot" ways of doing an effective follow up.
*   Failing to plan is planning to fail.

*   Two powerful secrets of making people work as a team.

*   Three strategies on how to re-sponsor distributors who have quit the MLM profession and _VOWED_ never to come back again!

If you examine the above topics very closely, you will definately realise that, they relate to serious matters which affect the business lives of all net work marketers world over. So if you position yourself as a "messiah" who can help them overcome their problems, they will flock to you in their large numbers as they perceive you as a priceless asset to them. That means free leads and endless business growth for you.

That's why there is a saying:

Help as many people as possible to get everything they want, yours will come automatically.

CHAPTER FOUR

FOUR ESSENTEALLY COMPONENTS FOR ATTRACTING: ENDLESS LEADS! MORE CASH! TO YOU

Y OU NEED THE FOLLOWING COMPONENTS TO KICK START THE DUPLICATIVE SPONSORING SYSTEM:

(i)   A web site where prospects can access your newsletter.
(ii) Promotion of your website through a comprehensive advertising campaign.
(iii) A newsletter of high value content, to do the "teaching" for you.
(iv) An autoresponder to hand over the newsletter to your prospects.

Website: you definately need a personal website where people can opt-in and request your news letter.

Promotion of website: it is vital that your website get advertised on different sites so that you can get enough exposure to your prospects(other net work marketers)and have a swarm of visitors into the website.

<u>Newsletter:</u> this is a very important information product that you can use to build a relationship with your prospects. It must contain a high quality educative message that will have an instant impact to its recepients(prospects) and yet short and to the point.

Long newsletters are hard to read because people naturally have a short corncetraction spurn. So it must be of reasonable length such that the person going through the newsletter, could just wish he/she continue reading it.

More importantly, the heading of your newsletter must capture the attention of the reader, because poor headings pisses people off. In other words give yourself enough time to prepare a concise and yet information "rich" newsletter.

<u>Note</u> I have given examples of attention capturing head lines for newsletters in the final page of chapter three.

<u>An autoresponder:</u> this is an internet mechanism that delivers your newsletter to your prospects. It keeps you connected to your audience(other net work marketers).

You must write messages that offer some *solutions(value)* to challenges faced by net work marketers, so that you are perceived as a professional advisor and an expert by your fellow colleagues. By so doing you will attract a huge number of information starved net work marketers to you and they shall look upon you for guiedance and leadership.

<u>CONSISTENCY</u>: Be consistent in producing and timenously delivering the newsletter to your prospects. This will make your target market(other net work marketers)realise that you were not 'KIDDING' when you say: you want to help them in running their MLM businesses.

Please make sure that at the end of your newsletter, you indicate your:

(i)   NAME.
(ii) CONTACT NUMBER.
(iii) WEBSITE ADDRESS.

*Now lets go a little bit further and MONETIZE THIS PROCESS, by introducing the:

SALEABLE INFORMATION PRODUCTS (S I P S)

The Duplicative sponsoring system, stipulates that you have to give your prospects some information products for free (such as newsletters), so that, you end up retailing, high value but reasonable priced products called (according to Mr Tshuma) the saleable information products (S I P S). These be could cds, videos, books etc.

Retailing of SIPS, help you to get instant cash that will fund more advertising campaigns.

*Suppose after giving a free newsletter say on PROSPECTING TIPS, you then suggest to your prospects that they can further enhance their knowledge on the same topic by buying on line a cheap but powerful cd/dvd.

I guarantee you that, they will be an overwhelming demand of your cd/dvd in question because prospects strongly believe in you as their distinguished business advisor. So, what ever you recommend to them to buy from you, they will just buy.

AS you continue giving your prospects valuable information about how best they can build their home based businesses and what to avoid, unexpectadly, you will get a suprise question like.

"So what business do YOU do?"

*Lets analyse, what is at the back of your prospect's mind that has triggered him/her to ask such a question.

It is possible that your prospect could think that, you could be a product of a successful and a highly reputable MLM company, because of the valuable educational information you have been given him/her. Therefore, the prospect feels it will be worth the candle to be part of your MLM company.

At this stage I can safely say, now bring your business opportunity into picture and gladly sponsor them.

CAUTION!! Not all your prospects(other net workers) will join your business opportunity. Perhaps 5% may request to be signed into your business, but the rest, which is 95% may remain loyal to their MLM companies but still continue buying your saleable information products as they see them useful to the growth of their businesses.

However, the GOOD news is that:

*YOU will continue making some serious CASH from people who have vowed NEVER to join your primary opportunity (which is likely to be 95% of the prospects) because they may choose to be loyal to their original companies, but however, remain the recepients of your informative newsletter and willing buyers of your S I P S.

Those prospects(the 95% who will never join your opportunity) may use your saleable information products (SIPS) (that contain your website)with their downlines in their respective MLM companies, and even recommend to their success lines about your excellence in mentoring other net work marketers, thereby giving you absolutely FREE advertisement of your website. That means MORE traffic generation for you!More leads!More business growth!

Say after a year or so take all your newsletters and compile them into a book that will be sold on line, so as to avoid the production and distribution expenses (you may sell hard copies, if you are financial able to do so). Perhaps, lets have a clear picture of the possible CASH that can be generated through this endeavor.

Retail your book, say for $30 per copy, and after a year or so, your website coud be possibly having over 25 000 subscribers(prospects whose email addresses are linked to your website).

Say 5% of the subscribers purchase the book within a month after it has been lauched, ie 10% of 25 000 people = 1250.

Then 1250 buyers x $30 per book = $37500, possible CASH for you! Period. End of story!

REMEMBER:

*   That the $37500 emnates from the initial sales volume which is associated with high demand caused by the lauch of the book, but expect more sales of this informative product as the years go by.
*   The sales of your book is not your only source of income, you still get income from makerting other SIPS like cds and videos on line, PLUS, the monthly BONUSES(pay checks) that you are paid by your primary MLM OPPORTUNITY!
*   Apart from giving you FREE advert or more exposure to your future prospects, the book will dramatically increase your _credibility ranking_ as an MLM expect which means: MORE leads, MORE cash, and incredible business growth!

* Say you also create an _affiliate link_ for each and every customer who purchases the book, and pay them say 20% commission for every person they reffer to buy the book through their affiliate link.

The "affiliate link" way of selling books will give you a fortune.

NOTE: The commission must be paid _only_ on ONE-LEVEL, so that you are not regarded as having started an MLM company. By so doing you are not putting yourself and those prospects who would have reffered others to buy the book, at risk of being at logger heads with their company policy as they will not be accussed of building a down line of another MLM company.

*A WELL MARKETED WEBSITE MEANS MORE CASH FOR YOU.

An extensively advertised personal website will attract swarms of free vistors into your site and, consequently, other people will pay you for allowing them to advertise on your site.

LINKING OF YOUR PERSONAL WEBSITE WITH YOUR MLM COMPANY WEBSITE.

Most of the MLM Companies create websites for each and every distributor/rep, within the company website. In that distributor's website, your customers can purchase products and join your MLM opportunity on line. It will be just as good as buying products or joining you directly. The monetery proceeds that emnate from such an internet transaction will be added to your monthly bonus by your MLM company. A pre-recorded business presentation will be included in the distributor's website.

So if your MLM company has such a facility, please, I urge you to link your personal prepared website with the website provided to you by your company, so that any of your prospects who request to join your MLM opportunity or want to buy the company products and probably need a presentation about business opportunity, may simple click the link that takes him/her directly to your company website. When he/she has opted into the company website, your prospects will easily access the business presentation and also order products on line.

Note:

The link to your MLM company website should be only exposed to the prospect when he/she has shown some interest in joining your primary opportunity.

WHAT ABOUT IF MY COMPANY DON'T HAVE SUCH A FACILITY:

Take advantage of YOU-TUBE(its a free video site) to upload a pre-recorded video of your company busines opportunity, which will always be accessible by those prospects who requested to join your opportunity. The business video must not be long, it must be reasonably short and yet having all the details.

LETS FAST FORWARD INTO THE FUTURE, SAY FIVE YEARS OR SO, OF USING THE DUPLICATIVE SPONSORING TECHNIQUES:

At this point you will find that your business will have grown beyond your wildest dreams. They will be thousands and thousads of people on your newsletter series, which means you may not be able to personal handle huge volumes of phone calls and responding to emails on a daily basis and hence the need to hire a personal secretary /assistant who will be helping you.

To pay those "employees" won't be a big deal because your business will be able to financially sustain itself by then.

There are companies that provide a service as personal assistant for other people/business organisations for a mothly fee or they may charge you small fee per call. The role of such a company is to respond to calls of your prospects on your behalf and also direct them step by step into your website.

This type of assistance carries two advantages:

*   Your work becomes easy because you are being assisted, which means that you now have quality time to do the most important thing in your business, which is follow ups and closing of business deals with your prospects.
*   Your CREDIBILITY RANKING will shoot up the roof, because when prospects call you its not you who respond but a personal secretary. So the prospects look at you as a serious business man of high integrity. That alone make people seek to do busines with you. NO MATTER WHAT!

This is in sharp contrast to uncle Tom, whom when prospects call, answers calls when he is at his house, whilst, in the background, there is noise from falling kitchen plates or worse still, there might be noise from crying children. Consequently, uncle Tom's image will be irrepairably damaged.

CREATION OF A DUPLICATIVE SPONSORING "UNIVERSITY"

After five years of running the duplicative sponsoring system, you would have acquired vast knowledge on internet net work marketing system, through reading of books and other relevant material. I suggest that, start your own "school", that will offer on line tutorial lessons to your prospects, that should also cover people who have already joined your primary opportunity. The duration of your on line courses, I suggest, must not be more than six months in length, just to keep them reasonably short.

"Is it necessary Mr. Tshuma to establish such a school when there is a book doing the teaching for me?"

Good question:

Here, we are applying the principles used at all educational institutions; they use both text books and live tutorial lessons. Remember, we are in the information marketing business. Most of the internet net work marketing big boys are already using this strategy and they are generating endless leads.

Your "Students" may contribute a monthly subscription to sustain the on line educational institution (monetization strategy in your favor). Please make sure that, your on line "students" get more knowledge that surpasses the subscriptions they are paying. In other words, OVER DELIVER!

<u>Do I still have to talk to people?</u>

People might think that, perhaps, phoning your prospects is no longer neccessary because of the internet strategies taught by the duplicative sponsoring system.

The person to person communication is extremely important in net work marketing. Talking to a real person can even eradicate fear on the side of the prospect, thinking that, may be it's a bogus business organisation they are being called for, and there could be a possibility of being ripped off.

Again, it is health for your business to develop strong relationships, through direct communication, with your prospects and leaders.

"but how do you do that, since the duplicative sponsoring approach makes people come to me without a single telephone call?"

There are some cases where talking to your audience is very neccessary. For instance, you need to connect directly with the prospects you have sponsored into your primary MLM opportunity.

So direct communication cements your relationship with your prospects, but in this case you will be interacting with people who have already pre-sold themselves to you.

MR TSHUMA I'M JUST NEW IN THE MLM INDUSTRY, I HAVE NO IDEA WHAT TO "TEACH" TO MY PROSPECTS:

Good question.

I would say that, even if you joined MLM today you can still give valuable information to other net work marketers.

Look for some people in your upline who are well versed with say:

* prospecting skills.
* Time management.
* Telephone skills.

And some other aspects of net work marketing, _interview_ these people, repackage the information, then send it to your tagert markert as your newsletter.

Secondly, I suggest that, you may approach the director of your MLM company and explain your overall strategy, then ask for permission to use their information products. Use, Only those pamphlets or cds that are motivational or that are generally teaching people about skills of running a home based business and not mentioning the name of your company. If your company grant you permission to use their material, go ahead and use it.

Many people in this industry including seasoned net work marketers have at one point in time followed the above path as a means of producing some marketing information.

GOLDEN ADVICE:

You don't have to be a rocket scientist to be able to implement the principles of duplicative sponsoring /attraction marketing. There is no need to write a book when you are new in attraction marketing philosophy.

*   What you should do, it's to:

(1) Create your website.
(2) Then, write simply but, content rich newsletters, which can be 10-15 lines on "hot" aspects of network marketing. For example, your newsletters may be crafted on the following topics:

*   The importance of goal setting.
*   Attitude determines your altitude.
*   Once you stop reading you stop leading!

     And many other simply but 'hot' topics that add value to the business lives of network marketers.

(3) Alternatively, as suggested earlier on, you have to record personal cds/videos or perhaps do some interviews with your well informed uplines on certain MLM aspects, then send that information as your newsletter.

(4)Make sure you attend your MLM company events and record powerful motivational speeches from your top leaders and may use such motivation as part of your newsletters or videos which prospects can download. In this case you must repackage the information such that, there is NO mentioning of your company name or its products, so as to avoid pitching your opportuniy to your prospects.

* By implementing these simple, but very poweful techniques, you will generate more leads and consequently, your business will grow progressively and systematically to higher and higher levels of income as you learn the duplicative sponsoring system.

Note:

You may employ this strategy during your early days in duplicative sponsoring system, but as time goes by, develop your own information content. Being creative is a PLUS to your personal image and business. This aspect shall be covered later in the book.

ADVANTAGES OF THE MONETZATION STRATEGY

(1) Funding your business activities becomes easy since you have generated enough cash flow through the monetization concept.
(2) Making instant cash by new distributors minimizes their chances of dropping out of business, as they are consistently encouraged by seeing the real fruits of their labour—which is cash in the pocket!
(3) Through the monetization endeavor you make money irregardless of whether people join your business or not, which therefore mean that, you are rewarded 100% for all your prospecting activities. Unlike a situation where one

uses the old school of network marketing, where you are NOT paid any penny if your prospect doesn't buy your Company products or business opportuniy.

(4) This strategy gives you multiple streams of income, thereby, ensuring that, you are now "immune" to the sudden drop in your MLM monthly checks caused by the distributors who become inactive or quit the business.

(5) Education marketing which result in the monetization process, positions you as a leader and a trustwothy MLM expect which make your people have an unwavering trust and loyality in you. That bond you have created with your prospects, can make the majority of them NOT to easily quit business.

(6) The other obvious advantage is that, you attract a lot of quality leads to yourself at the same time making money which means less stress and endless business growth.

(7) This system of marketing is automated 24/7, which means that it gives you ample time to do the most important business activity—which is follow up and sealing of business deals with your prospects.

Note:

*I did not state the disadvantages of monetization because there IS NO disadvantage in making money!

CHAPTER FIVE

THE SECRET OF RISING TO THE TOP POSITON IN YOUR MLM COMPANY

Apart from being focused, hard working, never giving up and not mingling with negative people, as always being said in most MLM company meetings. There is an easiest and the fastest way of rising to the top in your company.

The magic of success lies in creating your own content or information product rather than using someone else's content.

I remember very well my production and credibility ranking rose up sharply when I produced my "own" business dvd, and so was my income, and I moved quickly to a very senior and more rewarding position in the company's compensation plan. The dvd was just meant for me and my downlines but it had to spread like veld fire to other teams of my company who regarded it as a very useful tool for building their businesses. I made some thousands of dollars from the proceeds of the dvd because people demanded to buy the original copies from me, though, it was original not meant for sale. The biggest mistake I made was that, it was distributed off line, otherwise, I could have made a fortune from dvd sales and also attracted a huge number of prospects to me. But I always forgive myself for making such a blunder, because it were my dark days, I was completely not aware of the duplicative sponsoring system.

One day I went out for shoppinng at East Gate Mall in Johannesburg, South Africa. Then when I was busy picking my Grocery at Pick & Pay, a certain stranger approached me and said,

"Sorry brother, you look like somebody I know?"

I said "what?"

"Are you Mr Tshuma?"

I said "yes, you correct"

This man went on to tell me that he got to know me from the dvd that he had watched at his friend's place and loved the presentation so much. We exchanged business cards and after three days I sponsored him into the business, and he is one of most the active people in my team.

So many incidents of this nature happenned there after, which resulted in some people either joining the business or buying the products. Moreover, I got a lot of referrals from the people who had watched my dvd. What I noticed is that, through the dvd I had "branded" myself.

I encourage you to start producing small but useful educational information which can be in the form of newsletters, articles, your own videos . . . your own special report . . . . your own website where people can opt-in and request a piece of informative product.

Our job as MLM professionals is to produce and distribute information to our target market(other net work marketers). So show that you are creative by having original produced information, that will give you some "visibility" and it sets you head and shoulder above other distributors who only depend on company produced material. Remember people flock to people who have unique skills. So doing like the rest is not attractive.

The duplicative sponsoring system or the internet net work marketing has made it possible for distributors to differentiate themselves through giving people valuable MLM marketing material.

Lets take a look at the following messages that were used by two MLM professionals as they introduce their business on line, and draw a lesson from there:

Autopus Marketing:find how to add 7new reps per week without making a single call.

Systematic Attraction Marketing: stop cold calling and start getting prospects to call you.

These two attraction marketing professinals have written two different headings, but basically meaning the same thing. It's only that the writters are differentiating/ "branding" themselves.

Even companies create their own brand names such that customers can easily identify the company and it's products through it's brand.

In net work marketing you "brand" yourself by creating your own content that lead people to your website where they can access more information about what you offer.

Remember in chapter two of this book we said your business has nothing to do with your company which means that people JOIN YOU and not your company. Therefore, the educational content you produce "brands" you as the prospects align your credibility ranking to the quality of content that you personal produce. The higher your credibility ranking the more prospects you will attract to yourself.

Furthermore, for you to rise to the top in your MLM company, it means you have to perform far much better than any other distributor in your organisation. So your first job as a marketer is to position yourself against any competition. Whether you like it or not net work marketers compete for the attention of the prospects.

The more you learn the skills of how to out-wit your competitors, which are those thousands of distributors in your company, the higher the chances that you will rise to the top. The most powerful weapon that you can use to out play your competitors is to differentiate yourself through personal producing simple but high quality educational content which will instantly draw the attention of your prospects to YOU and consequently, make them ACT willingly on whatever you shall RECOMMEND.

*In the old school of net work marketing(referral system), it is difficult for people to rise to the top because distributors/reps are programmed to look the same, act the same, and say the same things as everyone else. It's like people reciting a poem, you can't identify the best voice as everyone is saying the same words in a simillar manner-there is no soprano, tenor, alto or bass, it's just the same monotonus voice. It's not attractive!

But, the duplicative sponsoring system is more liberal than the referral system. It allows people to convey the same message in different ways, because people create their own content to use as marketing tools. This allows distributors to differentiate and "brand" themselves, thereby, attracting more and more prospects to themselves, which ultimately leads to a huge business growth.

NOTE:

Producing quality educational content=Differentiation="Brand ing" yourself=surest way of rising to the top position in your MLM Company.

CHAPTER SIX

SUGGESTED SITES AND OTHER TOOLS FOR ADVERTISING YOUR BUSINESS

Some people who are obsessed by the idealogy of the old school of net work marketing, might argue and say advertising your businsess on the internet is very expensive visa-vie the less expensive ONE on ONE business presentations. These people "forget" to tell you that quality advertisements usually produces the best results and huge financial gains than those advertisements perceived otherwise.

*I might not touch all the sites where you may advertise your business but I will try my level best to highlight quite a number of such mass communication media.

NOTE:

You are NOT advertising your primary opportunity but you are advertising yourself and the expect help you want to render to your target market.

(a)   **Youtube.com**

* In Youtube you can upload your business video and promote an educational marketing message to a huge number of prospects. Which means you will be able to drive swarms of opportunity seekers and potential customers to your website to solicit for more information. (guess how much do you pay to use Youtube? . . . nothing!)

For your own information, over 14 million people watched the on line video in the US in December 2008.

* By using youtube you can be able to funnel a large number of potential customers and prospects from you tube to your website every single day.

(b) Twitter.com

* Twitter facilitates face to face networking, online social media . . . viral marketing . . .
* This powerful site allows you to interact with your prospects on a personal level.
* In Twitter you are able to respond to the questions of your prospects and update them on new products or promotions.
* It allows you to bond with your customers and easily direct them to your website.
* Twitter.com is free site, you pay nothing.

(c) Facebook.com

* Over 1000 000 people sign-up for facebook daily.
* Big companies use the facebook to sell, promote and effectively interact with their customers. So you can conduct an extensive advertising campaign on facebook. com

(d) Ezinearticles.com

* On this platform you can post very powerful business articles that will capture the attention of your audience, there by helping you to acquire instant authoriy and high credibilty ranking.
* You will zoom from being an amature to a highly recognised internet net work marketing coach.

(e) Google Adwords

* Google adwords is the fastest way to generate endless leads. There are no doubts about it.
* You simply have to sign for your own Google account, then create a "hot" ad that offers a solution to the problems faced by your target market. Then you will get a huge number of highly qualified prospects opting into your website to tap more information.

(f) Digg.com

* This is the most popular social news site on the planet.
* Digg.com has millions of monthly visitors than ABC, CBS, and FOX News . . .
* Just submit your story about what you offer to your target market. I can confidently assure you that your reputation "will shoot through the roof" and make your stuff ranked highly in the major search engines. Which means you will get more qualified leads.

(g) Lead Capture pages

* It gives you a plus to create your own LEAD CAPTURE PAGE because it sets you head and shoulder above your competitors.

* You have to craft your own powerful message and insert it on your lead capture page and immediately start interacting with your prospects.
* Your message should be unique, so that it can entice your prospects to willingly give you their contact info.

(h) Blogging

* A blog is a perfect place where you can engage with your targert market and easily convert them into customers.
* By providing useful educational information in your Blog, you can reap the benefit of that content being shared in the social media thereby helping to expose your website to more and more potential prospects.
* When you write useful educational information in your blog, prospect will not only visit the blog again and again, but they will also be enticed to:

  . buy your products.
  . To visit your website searching for more information
  . Fill out your lead capture pages.
  . Join your downline.

(i) Banner ads

* banner ads are more effective because, on a banner you can write a short but appealing message that can drive prospects into your website to search for more information.

Eg you may post message like:

"Hot" net work marketing tips

"Learn how to sponsor five or more people per week effortlessly"

For more info. _Click here_

This ad is directed to your target market (other net work marketers).

When reading this ad, people in net work marketing, particularly those who are struggling to sponsor new people into MLM opportunity will definitely CLICK, and opt into your website to solicit for more info.

Note: I could have gone on and on listing the marketing tools for your business, however, I have just given you a tip of the iceberg, so that you can realise that, by adopting the duplicative sponsoring / the attraction marketing strategy, you have so many tools at your disposal, to take your business to the next level.

CHAPTER SEVEN

HOW THE DUPLICATIVE SPONSORING SYSTEM SOLVES THE TWO MAJOR WOES OF MLM PROFESSIONALS

The duplicative sponsoring system/attraction marketing is a means for solving some of the problems faced in the net work marketing industry. Before we go any further lets briefly out line the two major problems that affect net work marketers and also, state suggested solutions vie the duplicative sponsoring system.

(1) Distributor/reps quit the MLM profession within 3months of joining the business.

The usually advice you get from your upline when a your downline quits the business is always "don't waste time Just REPLACE him and move on". No effort is made to determine the actual reasons that made the distributor to quit the business and then address the problem.

The funny thing is that, even if you "REPLACE AND MOVE ON" they will be a reoccurance of the same event because the majority of the newly recruited people to replace those who quit, will also quit. It's like filling water in a bucket that has holes underneath, hoping that it will eventually get full . . . total madness!

The permanent solution is to find the root cause of the problem rather than addressing the symptoms by saying "Replace and move on and stay focused"

One of the reason that make people to quit the MLM industry is that it takes time to develop a downline that can give you income to sustain your business. This is a painfully reality, whether you agree with me or not. After all, people join the net work industry mainly to achieve financial freedom and if they don't generate enough income within three months to six months, the usually reaction is retire forever back to their previous lives.

So new distributors quit the business, simply because they will be dead broke, as it takes a little bit of time to build a downline income that is enough to fund their business expenses.

"Whats the way forward Mr Tshuma since quiting the business of new distributors is a dangerous 'pandermic' in our industry?"

The only way to solve this problem is to create a markerting system that enables new and old distributors to immediately generate upfront retail profits which help them fund their primary business opportunity expenses and at same time generating endless leads for them. Believe you me, this technique will drastically reduce the number of people who drop out from the MLM industry before reaching their dreams.

Thanks to the internet and the duplicative sponsoring system because you will start making instant cash the very moment you plug into it. Which literally mean that people pay YOU for prospecting them.

NO MORE QUITERS ANY MORE!

(2) FEAR OF REJECTION

Fear of rejection was my serious enemy when I was new in this industry. To compound the problem, I was very shy, had little self esteem and I was dead broke.

I was that kind of a person who could do anything possible to avoid picking up phone and calling a prospect, because of fear that my cold market prospect could harshly turn me down.

This is a very serious problem affecting the MLM professionals, particularily the newly recruits. Fear of rejection is the major cause of down fall in this industry. As a newly recruited distributor, your first prospects are the people you know (warm market) that constitute friends, relatives and all the people who fall within your inner circle. The tendency is to approach these people with bubling confidence that they will instantly accept your business opportunity with open arms since they know you. Your hopes are dashed when you discover that they are not taking you serious about what you are saying to them, let alone accepting your business opportunity. This is a painful experience indeed, particularily if you are new in this profession.

Most of your uplines do not teach you how to get rid of rejection, but you are taught how to withstand it. Some uplines teach you that rejection is part of the game, so you must learn to "live" with it. It's like advising somebody to learn to live with a black mamba(snake) in his house because everyone is clueless about what do with it. The reason for saying so, its because uplines do not have a system that can completely get rid of rejection, but thanks to the attraction marketing system net work marketers can do their business in an environment that has a ZERO rejection, as people pre-sell themselves to you after they perceive you as a business consultant who teaches and guide them on how to run their businesses.

What is the root cause of rejection?

*The pitching of business opportunity/ product before educating prospects on information that add value to their business lives is the surest way of inviting rejection because as I said before:

> "people do not like to be sold anything but they like to buy anything as long as it has been their idea to do so"

*NOT knowing your targert market is another cause of rejection. The upline teaches that "everyone is a prospect" so you may go to everyone in the village telling them about your world class business opportunty, only to discover that people do not need what you are selling, that's why they are giving you a cold shoulder. Its like selling red meat to the vegetarians or selling alchohol to the Seventh Day Adventist Church members. Its a loose-loose situation because you are selling a wrong product to the wrong people . . . because of the wrong assumption that everyone is a prospect.

The only solution to this puzzle is to use the duplicative sponsoring system, it mentors you on how to identify your targert markert and how to take your message to your prospects. It will link you directly with the people who actually want to talk to you, who respect what you do and are more than willing to do what you are doing.

*NOT knowing what you are selling is another major cause of rejection. You are not selling what you think you are selling.

What is it that we are suppose to be selling?

It is not your company products /business opportunity that you are selling, but it is **YOU** the product you are selling to your targert market. As discussed earlier, you sell your expertise to other net work marketers on how they can run their business better. By so doing you play the role of a trustworthy consultant not a salesman. Your business opportunity must feature in, as a BACK END product which is likely to be willingly accepted by your prospects, because you have earned the right to sell them your opportunity through educating them first before pitching sales. That's how you can avoid rejection using the duplicative sponsoring system.

CHAPTER EIGHT

THE IMPORTANCE OF EFFECTIVE FOLLOW UP TECHNIQUES IN ATTRACTION MARKETING

Sending a newsletter to your prospects, helps to you create a cordial business relationship with them. However, the resultant relationship should be gently natured through an effective follow up mechanism till the prospect make a decision to purchase either the:

(1) saleable information product.(SIPS) or
(2) Business opportunity.

Or both the SIPS and the business opportunity.

*Please note that, the relationship with your prospects is PERMANENT, which therefore mean that, even if your prospects buy(doesn't buy) the products you offer, you have to keep connected to them through newsletters because he/she may reffer someone to you, or the prospect might decide to buy your products in the near future and this is health for your business.

The follow up process may reveal the following characteristics traits of the distributor/rep:

(a) <u>The poverty mentality or "failure mindset"</u>

*This type of mindset is shown when a distributor is very desparate to sign up a prospect, because he/she feels that without sponsoring a new recruit he is not going to make some money, consequently, he won't be able to pay his bills, so he has no choice, but to literal beg the prospect to join the MLM opportunity.

The decision to stoep so low to the extent of begging a prospect to join your MLM opportunity shows that the distributor has emotionally attached himself to the sponsoring process, such that the he/she may quit the business if the prospect doesn't take up the business opportunity.

I used to experience such challenges during my early years in net work marketing, but thanks to the creation of duplicative sponsoring system things changed overnight, now I'm being sought after by my prospects ready to join my primary opportunity. You can also enjoy the same benefits if you take the advice given in this book very seriously.

Note:

No one is interested in being sponsored by a desperate person. Unfortunately, it's so sad to realise that a frightening number of the net work markers have adopted the poverty mentality route when sponsoring new reps, and that explains why 80% of the net work marketers fail to prosper in this industry.

(b) <u>The abundance mentality or "success mindset"</u>

*This state of mindset occurs when you tell yourself that you are not needy, everything will come natural to you; at the right time. You tell yourself that, when the time is ripe you shall have more money . . . more leads . . . more prosperity, because you are no longer driven by a mentality of scarcity.

When you have an abundance mentality, you are not affected by the stress caused by the lack of money or failure to sponsor new distributors. This type of mind set will earn you respect from your prospects because you are giving them space to decide whether to join you or not. You are not imposing your business opportunity on them. This increases your value to others, it gives you power and generate attraction.

*So an effective follow up occurs when a distributor/rep demonstrate an abundance mentality to his/her prospects.

*At this point let's examine two follow up emails sent by net work marketer to a potential prospect that has requested to join the MLM opportunity.

(1) "Hey Peter, it's David Michaels. I have just sent you a distributor application form; please feel free to fill in the necessary details and when you are done, just give me a call.

This is a very weak email because it shows that David Michaels is extremely desperate to sponsor Peter. That's why David is using persuasive words "please feel free" as if Peter is being begged to sign the distributor application form. Secondly, there is no specific time frame set for Peter to sign and email the distributor application form back to David Michaels. The impression given in this whole scenario is that, if Peter is politely told when to submit the form, he might decide otherwise. So David Michaels is afraid that he might lose his one and only prospect Peter.

Such type of emails suddenly make a prospect think you can't do your business without him and therefore he is pivotal to your success. The prospect have absolutely nothing to lose and the business deal will be decided on the prospect's terms. The chances are high that the prospect might not join your primary opportunity as you are perceived to be valueless.

(2) *"Hey Peter, its David Michaels. I have just sent you a distributor application form. Fill in the necessary details and email it to me within two days. If ever there are questions don't hesitate to call me on 0217463 or send me an email. I will gladly answer your questions.*

Wish you the best.

The second email shows that David Michaels is in control of the sponsoring process. He precisely gives Peter the instructions as to what should be done as far as filling in of the form is concerned. David Michaels sets the time frame for submission of the distributor application form, "within two days"

Here, David is demonstrating that; he is a leader because leaders give instructions and he also indirectly tell Peter that, time is very important, which is the most important quality of a serious businessman.(abundance mentality)

"Which is the most important activity in net work marketing?"

The are so many possible answers that can be given in an attempt to answer this question. However; the most crucial activity in net work marketing, according to my point of view, it's FOLLOW UP.

"Why Mr Tshuma?"

Simply because, in many cases, people make buying decisions of your product/opportunity after a follow up process. In making a follow up you take orders and make money.

So the more follow ups you make the more orders you get. The more money you make. Suggesting that, you must spend 50% of your time in doing an effective follow up, if you want to make serious cash in this industry.

The table below shows how most of MLM professionals spend their business time.

Activity	Time Allocation	Monetery Gain
Prospecting	60%	Nothing
Training	30%	Nothing
Making Follow up calls	10%	Yes you make money

If you look at this table closely, it tells you that people spend most of their time on activities that that don't give them money(though those activities are very important), which is the reason why most people do not make it in the MLM profession.

"So what's the way forward because for you to make a follow up you should have firstly done some prospecting?"

Good Question:

* I know it's a bit difficult to balance up your business activities in favour of allocating 50% of your time to follow up. So I suggest that, adopt the duplicative sponsoring system which is automated 24/7, and can run on it's own without your direct interference(but don't forget to feed the system with newsletters) and thereby creating ample time

to do your most important activity . . . follow up which gives you orders=cash into your pocket.

*   Secondly, as suggested in chapter four of this book, you may hire the services of a call centre company which will act as your personal assistant. The role of such a company is to answer calls of the prospects on your behalf 24/7 and to direct them into your websites. This service will not only create enough time for you to do the follow up service, but will also increase your credibility ranking to unprecedented levels, simply because of the fact that you have a personal assistant, therefore, you will be perceived as a successful businessman worth to do business with. You can be in a position to do this, when your business is generating over $10 000 per month.

REMEMEBER:

If there is no sale/orders nothing happens in business.

READ this statement again.

The table below shows the suggested time allocation for your business activities.

Activity	Time Allocation	Monetery Gain
Prospecting	30%	Nothing
Training	20%	Nothing
Making Follow Up Calls	50%	Yes you make money

YOU may produce your own time allocation schedule, but make sure that, the follow up process get the bulk of your time.

CHAPTER NINE

TAKE CHARGE OF THE DUPLICATION PROCESS

After directly sponsoring say 10 to 15 distributors/reps don't relax and expect your down lines to recruit new people for you. Not everyone will duplicate you. So you have to assume full responsibility for your business growth.

Horizontal growth:

In net work marketing we have what is called horizontal growth, which occurs when you personal sponsor first line distributors. These are distributors that were personal signed by you when they were initial joining the business. I can safely say that, the first line distributors are the most important pillars of your business, because when these people reach the higher levels within the compensation plan of your MLM Company, you automatically get promoted to higher and more rewarding levels of your Company.

Vertical growth:

This growth occurs when your team recruit/sponsor new people. In other words these are 2nd, 3rd, and 4th . . . generation of your team.

*Do not rely only on the new people brought by your team members, because this promotes vertical growth of your business which might bring severe consequences in the long run.

What do I mean by this?

Too much dependency on certain team members to do the sponsoring of new distributors for you might imply that your monthly pay check is now dependent on the sales volume of one or two highly productive members of your team. This is a very dangerous situation in your business because the very person you were dependent on might quit the business taking a huge sales volume with him. It means you will become a destitute in a twinkle of an eye.

I have seen such bad occurrences happening to many people in this industry, where you find someone who has been regarded as a shining star of the team, all of a sudden turns into a shooting star and disappear forever, leaving the sponsor with tears running down the cheeks . . . miserable!

So the more you personal sponsor new people, the more you safe guard your business, the more you compound your growth and the more you will reach your goals quickly.

So strikes a balance, by promoting both the horizontal and the vertical growth, so that there is stability in your team. You have to lead by example. Your people have to practical see you in action of sponsoring new reps /distributors, so that they can follow your foot steps

Remember in order to develop and attract leaders, you must become one yourself. Be a role model to your team. ***People never do what you preach, but they do what you practice!***

CHAPTER TEN

MY FINAL REMARKS

Entrepreneurs "see" opportunities in their minds, that other people fail to "see" with their eyes wide open.

I strongly believe that, by mere purchasing of this book, you have an entrepreneur mindset, you have a burning desire for success, therefore, take advantage of the attraction secrets taught in this book and dilligently apply them in your business. Believe, it will work for you as it has worked for others. The attraction system is pretty quicker in producing the desired results, as long as it is implemented correctly.

Certainly, it doesn't matter how much "never giving up" you are in trying to take down a concreate hall with your bare head, the honest truth is that, it will never fall. The more you try, the more painful it shall become, the more frustrated you shall feel. In otherwords, doing the wrong things consistently, will never yield positive results irregardless of your persistence in doing it. So, why? Should you cling to an old system of network marketing when you know very well that it promotes pitching of sales, which literally chases prospects away from you.

A certain philosopher, once said:

> "I will rather die for an idea that will live than to live for an idea that will die"

It might sound difficult at first, to implement the strategies taught in the duplicative sponsoring system, but, it is worth it, to take a decision and get started by creating a simple website and little by little start writing some newsletters and send them to your prospects. You can just send one newsletter per week and be consistent in doing this, and be rest assured that within a short space of time you will start receiving some emails from your prospects passing comments about the material you are teaching them and that may mark the beggining of a relationship building process leading to the buying of your SIPS and eventually signing up of the prospects into your primary MLM opportunity.

*Imagine owning a marketing system that can talk to 50, 100, 2000, or more people on your behalf, every single day, without your direct involvement. It delivers your message intact without distortion over and over again to every prospect. It never stops. It never get tired. It never get sick of saying the same message.

*Having said that, the marketing system is automated, working 24/7, that doesn't mean that you have to sit back and relax because the internet is doing the work for you. The fact of the matter is that network marketing is about building relationships. Consequently, personal interaction and coaching of your team is the glue that cements your organization together.

The marketing system will go half way in getting the highly qualified leads that need what you offer and then you have to play the other half by making a vigorous follow up and ensure that you manage the sponsoring process until the prospect finally sign the distributor joining form. It doesn't end there, you still have to train/ mentor your team on how to use the duplicative sponsoring system in their MLM businesses. You have to help your team succeed by developing leaders. The automated machines can't do that for you. But the good news is that, the job of mentoring your team becomes easy because of the use of the attraction marketing system.

Do not be **DECEIVED** by thinking that you will never make a phone call to your prospects as long as you are using the attraction marketing system. I would like you to understand that, human beings are social beings, they need to interact with each other and nothing can fill in the vaccum of person to person interaction. It's our natural survival instinct. So calling your prospects it's an integral part of the duplicative sponsoring system.

Please, do not think that I'm now contradicting myself by saying that we have to make phone calls to our prospects. Let me clear the dust by indicating the role that will be played by the duplicative sponsoring system and the part you will have to play in the process. The duty of the duplicative sponsoring is to 'separate the wheat from chaff' that is giving you, only the serious prospects who already need what you offer. Now your role is to close the business deal, through calling highly qualified prospects who have already pre-sold themselves to you. Here, you are not convincing the prospects of anything, but you are just leading them through sponsoring process until they sign the distributor application form (ie until they join your primary opportunity).

I hope you can see the difference between calling "everybody" as what happens when you are using the trditional approach to net work marketing and only calling highly qualified prospects who desparately need what you offer, as is the case with the duplicative sponsoring system.

That's why Ann Sieg had this to say

"And because of the trends of doing business on the internet is not talking with people, **combining** real human interaction with automated system can become a very powerful angle to take that few others are using"

On another note, I know you have been told by your MLM companies that if you are failing in this industry its because you lack belief in the power of net work marketing or you are failing because you are not self motivated or your "why" you joined the business is too "small" and that's the reason you are doing badly in this industry. Yes, that could be true to a certain extent, but however, I would like to dismiss this opinion as absolutely hogwash.

Personal I think people fail to achieve their dreams because of the fact that, they do this business with ineffective marketing tools that mainly focus on how good their MLM company products are (i,e pitching sales) and less focus is given to what the prospect think about the product being offered to him/her, forgetting that the "buying" decision lies mainly with the prospect at the end of the day.

You can have the biggest "why" in the world . . . you can be highly motivated distributor in your company but as long as you are using the wrong techniques nothing will ever change. For instance, I have seen MLM professionals chasing strangers in malls, stopping people who are doing shopping, telling them "you look businessman like, I have a business that you can do"

The first impression that is created by this approach is that, you are being addressed by some kind of a coneman, then guess the response?

So its high time people stop using these harrassing methods or "interruption marketing" as a strategy of prospecting, because this lead to failure and is out dated. The answer to this problem lies in adopting a marketing system that will get customers / prospects to talk to you first ready to buy what you are offer.

The old school of net work marketing of cold calling leads, buying leads that have been sold to twenty other people and knocking on people's doors trying to show them the opportunity is now "out of fashion"

*By using the duplicative sponsoring system, you can immediately start attracting swarms of leads to you, who will actually pay you for showing them the business opportunity.

*The naked truth is that, we are living in the internet age and there is NO going back on this technologically advancement. So if someone is opposed to the leverage provided by the internet, its like opposing the tsunami waters, you will be swept off and be part of statistics of people who never made it MLM.

*Remember:

The secret of success in this industry lies in marketing smarter not selling harder.

This is what the duplicative sponsoring system is all about. The system helps you to create a customer base through retailing inexpensive but highly valuable information products (SIPS), thereby generating instant cash for you and at the same time giving you the opportunity to smoothly "drive" these satisfied customers to buy your back-end product(business opportunity).

It is easy to offer your business opportunity to customers who have bought your SIPS, because you taught them, through your information products, how to run an MLM business prior to joining one. So by teaching them first before joining the business opportunity, you would have completely destroyed one major cause of FEAR Which is **lack of knowledge** on how to run a successful MLM business.

You must be a doer!

Walk the talk, put into practice what you have learnt in this book. This is the most important qualification that distinguish winners from losers.

Never procastinate and say:

> "I will start tomorow or next year or when I have read an enough number of books"

I urge you not to post pone your success. You have learnt information that is enough to kick start your own duplicative sponsoring programme.

START NOW!

WHAT'S HOLDING YOU BACK?

If people don't find a reason to follow you, they will definately follow someone else. And they are many people out there, who are more than ready to be followed.

"Hay whilst the sun still shines"

I wish you all the best on your path to success!

Nqobile Tshuma

CEO:

THE DUPLICATIVE SPONSORING SYSTEM.

www.duplicativesponsoring.com